ALLIGATORS

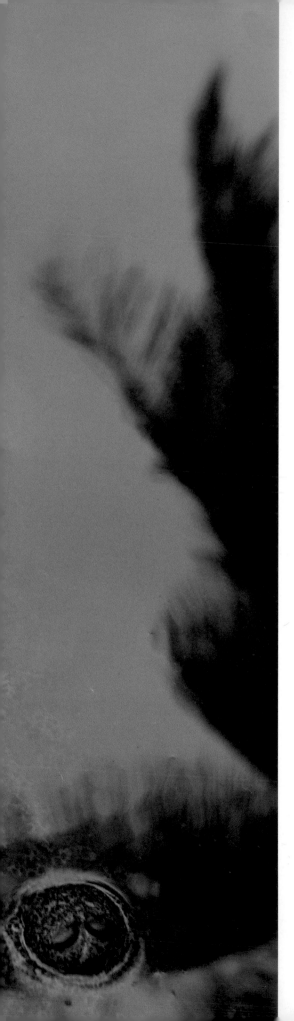

LIVING WILD

Published by Creative Education
P.O. Box 227, Mankato, Minnesota 56002
Creative Education is an imprint of The Creative Company
www.thecreativecompany.us

Design and production by Mary Herrmann
Art direction by Rita Marshall
Printed by Corporate Graphics in the United States of America

Photographs by Alamy (Blickwinkel, David Sanger Photography, David Hosking, North Wind Picture Archives, Vespasian), Corbis (China Photos/Reuters, Philip Gould), Dreamstime (Norman Bateman, Mike Brown, Gary Bydlo, Rusty Dodson, Zheng Dong, Bruce Dowlen, Russell Du Parcq, James Elliott, Frenta, Martin Muransky, Nouubon, Marek Slusarczyk, Brandon Smith), Getty Images (Tim Chapman, Willard R. Culver/National Geographic, Norbert Rosing), iStockphoto (Ross F. Bass, Tony Campbell, Ovidiu-Mihai Dancaescu, Tom Delme, Mark Higgins, Stefan Klein, Eberhard Kraft, Elizabeth Kratzig, Robert Linton, Diana Lundin, Matt Matthews, Darryll Mills, Bill Stamatis, Nicola Stratford, Tomasz Szymanski, Rudi Tapper, Scott Winegarden)

Library of Congress Cataloging-in-Publication Data
Gish, Melissa.
Alligators / by Melissa Gish.
p. cm. — (Living wild)
Includes bibliographical references and index.
Summary: A look at alligators, including their habitats, physical characteristics such as their scaly skin, behaviors, relationships with humans, and threatened status in the world today.
ISBN 978-1-58341-967-0
1. Alligators—Juvenile literature. I. Title. II. Series.

QL666.C925G55 2010
597.98'4—dc22   2009025168

CPSIA: 092611 PO1507

9 8 7 6 5 4 3

CREATIVE EDUCATION

ALLIGATORS

Melissa Gish

Mosquitoes hover over a craggy log as it floats in a pool of murky water. A group of yellow-bellied slider

turtles, lined up on a fallen tree near the water's edge, warm themselves in the late afternoon sun.

osquitoes hover over a craggy log as it floats in a pool of murky water. A group of yellow-bellied slider turtles, lined up on a fallen tree near the water's edge, warm themselves in the late afternoon sun. A white ibis, its feathers bright and glistening, steps lazily along the shore, stooping to pluck snails from the mud with its long beak. One of the turtles slips from its perch to take a swim. It paddles in slow circles,

then drifts near the craggy floating log. To the turtle's surprise, the log comes to life—an alligator! With a sudden splash, the alligator thrashes its head to one side and grabs the turtle in its jaws, crushing its shell. Then it raises its head out of the water and lets the meal slide down its throat, gulping once, twice, . . . and the turtle is gone. Settling back into stillness, the alligator awaits its next unwary prey.

WHERE IN THE WORLD THEY LIVE

■ **American Alligator**
southeastern United
States

■ **Chinese Alligator**
along China's lower
Yangtze River

The two species of alligator are found in distinct
regions of the world, with the Chinese alligator
limited to China's lower Yangtze River and the
American alligator prevalent among the swamps,
rivers, and lakes of the southeastern United States.
The colored squares represent the common
locations of each species.

MUDDY DRAGON

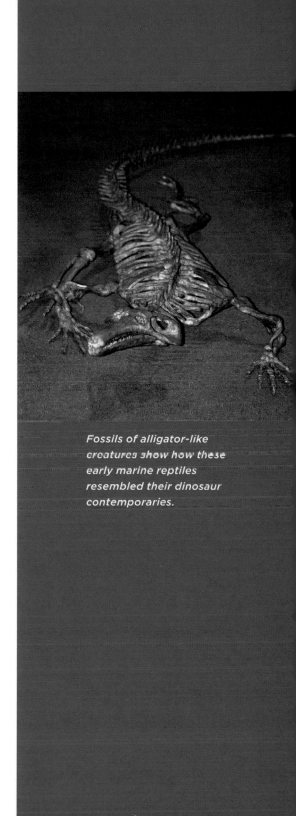

W ith the exception of their size, alligators have changed little since the last days of the dinosaurs, and scientists refer to alligators and their relatives—crocodiles, caimans, and gharials— as living fossils. There are two species of alligator, the American alligator (*Alligator mississippiensis*) and the Chinese alligator (*Alligator sinensis*). The word "alligator" comes from the Spanish *el lagarto,* meaning "the lizard." Spanish explorers who reached Florida in the 1500s called the giant, lizard-like creature they discovered there *el lagarto.* In its native land of China, the Chinese alligator has traditionally been nicknamed the "muddy dragon."

Alligators are reptiles. Reptiles are ectothermic animals, meaning that their bodies depend on external sources of heat, and their temperatures change with the environment. In the morning and late afternoon, alligators leave the water and come on to land to warm their bodies in the sun. At midday, when the sun becomes stronger, they retreat to the water to prevent overheating. They sleep at night while floating in the water. Like most reptiles, alligators reproduce by laying eggs.

Fossils of alligator-like creatures show how these early marine reptiles resembled their dinosaur contemporaries.

Differences between alligators and crocodiles can be seen in the teeth.

Alligators bellow to attract mates and define territories; their hearing is good, and they can hear calls on land up to 165 yards (150 m) away.

Alligators are closely related to and often confused with crocodiles. The main differences between the two reptiles are found by observing the head. When a crocodile's mouth is closed, an enormous fourth tooth on the lower jaw juts up behind its nostrils. But the fourth tooth of an alligator is located inside a hollow spot in the alligator's upper jaw, so when its mouth is closed, all of its teeth are hidden. Also, all crocodiles have narrow, V-shaped snouts, but alligators have wide, U-shaped snouts.

The alligator's dark green body is covered with thick, scaly skin. Under the skin of the back and tail are protective bony ridges called scutes. Tiny pits in the skin called **dermal** pressure receptors cover the alligator's upper and lower jaws. These organs make the alligator highly sensitive to changes in water pressure and movement of prey. When a fish swims nearby or an animal touches its mouth to the water's surface for a drink, the tiny waves of movement that are created alert the alligator to the precise location of the prey, even in darkness.

The earliest alligator ancestor was a chicken-sized reptile that lived on land more than 200 million years ago. Alligator ancestors became **aquatic** about 160 million

Using their powerful tails, alligators will propel themselves out of the water to snap at low-flying birds.

Highly secretive Chinese alligators will hide for up to half the year in underground burrows.

years ago. Fossil remains show that several alligator ancestors grew to lengths of more than 50 feet (15.2 m). Modern alligators are not nearly as large. Male American alligators average about 13 feet (3.9 m) in length and weigh 800 pounds (363 kg), but they are capable of reaching 18 feet (5.5 m) and more than 1,000 pounds (454 kg). Females are always smaller than males and rarely grow to be more than 10 feet (3 m) long.

Much smaller than the American alligator, the Chinese alligator averages about 5 feet (1.5 m) in length and weighs up to 90 pounds (41 kg). The Chinese alligator's snout, slightly upturned and more tapered, is different from the American alligator's. And unlike the American alligator, the Chinese species has a bony plate on its belly as well as a bony plate on each upper eyelid. These features help protect the Chinese alligator as it burrows in the earth during winter months.

The Chinese alligator, mentioned in stories dating back to A.D. 200, was once common in both northern China's Yellow River and the Yangtze River, which flows from central China to the southern part of the country. Today, however, most of the remaining wild population of fewer than 200 alligators is limited to an area of about 167 square miles (433 sq km) along the lower Yangtze River.

American alligators can be found in much greater numbers. Half a million years ago, when much of the

Adult alligators can survive two years without eating and will fight over food only when they are very hungry.

Swinging its tail while high-walking propels an alligator forward at a much faster speed than its normal rate.

southern United States was swampland, the American alligator ranged from Mexico to Florida and as far north as Oklahoma and Virginia. Today, it can be found only in swamps, rivers, and lakes in the southeastern U.S., with the highest populations occurring in Louisiana (about 1.5 million), Florida (about 1 million), and Georgia (about 200,000).

Alligators, North America's largest reptiles, now compete for food with pythons that have been introduced to their wetland habitats.

An alligator can move swiftly on land by lifting its body and part of its tail and running on its toes, a technique called high-walking. Alligators can sprint about 11 miles (17.7 km) per hour—as fast as most human beings— for about 30 yards (27.4 m) before tiring. However, an alligator's body is designed for swimming. In the water, its **webbed** feet are tucked close to its body, and its tail, which makes up half of its body length, moves back and forth to propel the animal tirelessly through the water. An alligator is so strong that it can throw itself five feet (1.5 m) onto shore to seize prey.

Alligators have five claws on each front foot and four on each back foot. They use their claws to dig holes and tunnels, and females build nests on which they can lay their eggs. Alligators also use their claws to hold prey

An alligator's transparent inner eyelid closes back-to-front, while its outer lid closes top-to-bottom.

Alligators are opportunistic feeders and will lie perfectly still underwater or hidden in vegetation for hours while waiting for prey.

to the ground or underwater, where they spend most of their time. By adjusting the amount of air in its lungs, an alligator can float or submerge at will. When an alligator goes underwater, folds of skin close over its ears; muscles seal its nostrils shut; and its tongue, which is attached to the bottom of its mouth, works like a plug to block water from the throat.

Like many **vertebrates**, such as cats, the alligator has a layer of tissue called a tapetum lucidum behind each retina, the light-sensitive part of the inner eye. The tissue, which improves the animal's night vision, results in light being reflected off the eyes, an effect called eyeshine. In addition, a nictitating (*NIK-tih-tayt-ing*) membrane (a see-through inner eyelid) closes over the alligator's eyes for protection underwater.

Alligators are carnivores, meaning they eat meat. They typically need to eat only once or twice a week. Adult alligators have as many as 80 teeth in their jaws, but they do not chew their food. Rather, they tear off chunks of meat and swallow them whole. Their bite force is one of the strongest in nature, and once captured, their prey seldom escapes.

Scientists concerned about human consumption of alligator meat first study the health of the fish that alligators eat.

Mating alligators may first cross paths in a weedy, low-lying area, but they require open water for courtship rituals.

READY TO HUNT

An alligator's maturity has more to do with size than age. Alligators are ready to mate when they are about six feet (1.8 m) long. Males typically grow faster and reach this size at an earlier age than females. Reptiles in general develop more quickly in heat than in cold, and an alligator reaches breeding size in seven to nine years in a warm climate. However, alligators that live in cooler climates may not reach six feet (1.8 m) for up to 19 years. A female who is ready to breed will establish herself in a heavily vegetated marsh for the remainder of her life, waiting for suitable males to find her. **Solitary** males establish territories in areas of open water and travel long distances to find mates.

The mating season occurs between April and July, but not every female breeds every year. When a female accepts a male partner, their courtship begins with a touching of snouts. Then the pair swims to open water that is at least six feet (1.8 m) deep, where they engage in an activity called "head slapping." Each alligator rests its lower jaw on the surface of the water and then slaps down its upper jaw, causing a loud pop as the jaws meet.

Dense, fast-growing water hyacinth, also known as alligator weed, is present in about 80 percent of alligator habitats.

The yellow stripes on an alligator hatchling help it blend in among swamp grasses and rays of sunlight.

To communicate with each other, the alligators exhale bubbles of air from their nostrils and bellow. A male will repeat this performance with the same female many times during a season.

The female begins building her nest two to three weeks after the male has returned to his territory. She seeks a spot near water that is on higher ground and uses her claws and snout to rake soil, leaves, and sticks into a mound about six feet (1.8 m) in diameter and three feet (.9 m) high. She lays an average of 35 leathery-shelled eggs on the mound and then covers them with about 1 foot (30.5 cm) of vegetation.

The rotting vegetation creates heat, which keeps the eggs warm for about 65 days. The amount of heat created will determine the gender of the offspring. Within the first 21 days, temperatures below 86 °F (30 °C) will produce females, but temperatures higher than 93 °F (34 °C) will produce males. Temperatures between those two limits can produce either female or male offspring.

As a baby alligator grows inside its egg, an egg tooth develops on the tip of its snout. This sharp projection of skin enables the hatchling to slice through the egg's

Mother alligators and their offspring remain close to their wetlands nesting site after the babies hatch.

Hatchlings claw their way up to ride on their mother's back, enjoying her protection for up to three years.

leathery interior membrane and break the shell. This egg tooth is resorbed into the body within a week of hatching. Incredibly, each three-inch-long (7.6 cm) egg holds a hatchling that is six to eight inches (15–20 cm) long.

Female alligators guard their nests and are usually present at hatching time. A mother may carry her young to water, but instinct ultimately prompts the hatchlings to move from the dry darkness of the nest toward sunshine and water. For the first few days of their lives, the young continue to be nourished by the egg yolk still attached to their bodies. But the sharp-toothed and alert alligators are immediately equipped to hunt for prey, which includes crayfish, insects, and small fish.

The mother alligator keeps her offspring close for about five months. Then the group, called a pod, will leave her but remain together in the same place for one to two years. During this time, their numbers will be reduced by 80 percent, as wild cats, otters, turtles, catfish, and large wading birds such as herons prey upon them. The greatest threat to young alligators is posed by older alligators, which are responsible for 50 percent of hatchling deaths.

Within their first year, hatchlings grow to 24 inches (61 cm) in length. In each of the next 3 years, these juveniles add another 12 inches (30.5 cm). Only about 17 percent of a season's hatchlings ultimately survive to reach the age of 4, an age at which the alligators are no longer vulnerable to predators. From then on, they will have few enemies other than larger alligators and humans.

Alligators grow rapidly until they are eight years old and about eight feet (2.4 m) long. At that point, their growth rate slows down considerably and is affected more by climate. Alligators grow faster when temperatures are between 85 and 91 °F (29 to 33 °C). When the surrounding temperature drops below 70 °F (21 °C), alligators may stop eating, and their growth ceases.

Yet alligators can tolerate cold better than extreme heat. In places where temperatures fall below 55 °F (13 °C), such as in the habitat of Chinese alligators, the alligators will dig burrows and enter a sleeplike state called brumation, remaining motionless for months. Even if it is trapped in ice with only its snout exposed to the

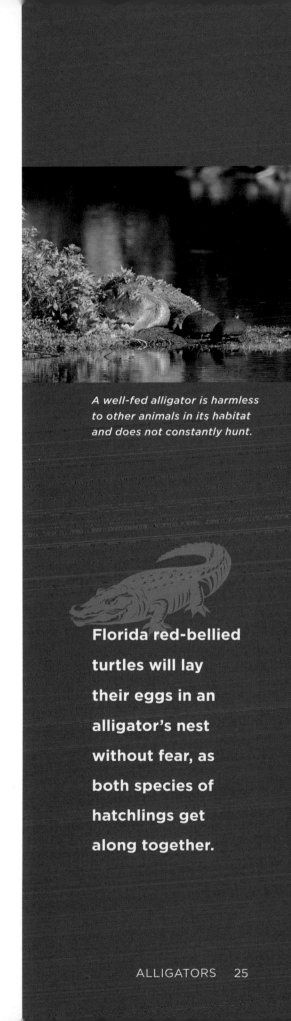

A well-fed alligator is harmless to other animals in its habitat and does not constantly hunt.

Florida red-bellied turtles will lay their eggs in an alligator's nest without fear, as both species of hatchlings get along together.

During dry times, alligators are forced to stay near their gator holes, where food is scarcer.

The oldest living American alligator is 72-year-old Muja, who arrived at Serbia's Belgrade Zoo in 1937, one year after the zoo's founding.

air, an alligator can survive with a body temperature that is half of its ideal temperature of 81 °F (27 °C). On the other hand, if an alligator gets too hot and is unable to cool off, it will suffer and die.

Alligators are vital to the survival of other animals living in their habitats. Adult alligators create and expand areas called "gator holes" over a period of many years, using snouts and claws to first clear out plants from an area, then thrashing their bodies and tails around to dig out depressions. These holes fill with water during the wet season and hold water after the rains stop. When water is scarce elsewhere, gator holes provide a shared water source for alligators, fish, birds, and other animals.

An alligator often expands its gator hole by digging tunnels. Up to 60 feet (18.3 m) long, an alligator tunnel ends in a burrow with a ceiling high enough above the water level to allow the alligator to breathe. Inside these burrows, alligators can survive dry seasons or harsh winters. In the wild, alligators can live about 50 years, but kept safe and well fed in captivity, they can live up to 80 years.

Alligators share their habitats with wading birds such as storks, spoonbills, herons, and great white egrets.

Monstrous reptiles historically symbolized evil, and in myths and legends, heroes were called upon to slay them.

EARTH TREMBLERS

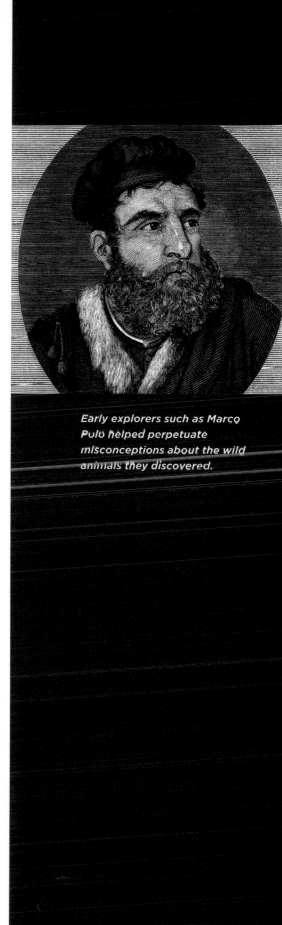

Medieval tales of fire-breathing dragons owe much of their popularity to Chinese alligators, which were first described to Europeans by the Italian explorer Marco Polo in the 13th century. For hundreds of years after that, Europeans regarded alligators and crocodiles as fearful sea monsters of legendary proportions, nearly impossible to kill.

When 16th-century European explorers began traveling to the New World of the Americas, alligators were captured and sent back to Europe to be sold to wealthy people who collected exotic animals. In 1682, French explorers in Louisiana even sent an alligator to their king, Louis XIV, who immediately ordered his scholars to study the strange creature. These early encounters with American alligators became the subject of horror stories that persisted for generations.

In his 1791 book, *Travels*, American naturalist William Bartram vividly described a scene of alligators feeding on trout, with "floods of water and blood rushing out of the mouths, and the clouds of vapour issuing from their wide nostrils." Bartram also wrote about one particularly large

Early explorers such as Marco Polo helped perpetuate misconceptions about the wild animals they discovered.

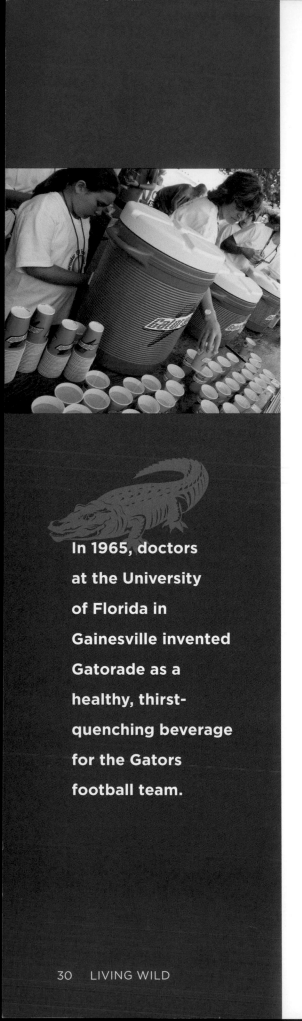

In 1965, doctors at the University of Florida in Gainesville invented Gatorade as a healthy, thirst-quenching beverage for the Gators football team.

alligator, saying, "The earth trembles with his thunder." Equally as lavish were the alligator stories that came from the American Indians of the Southeast.

While many southern tribes hunted alligators for the animals' meat and skins, they also incorporated these reptiles into their religious views. As Europeans journeyed across the southern U.S., they came upon people who respected and sometimes even worshiped alligators. The Bayougoula people, who lived on the western banks of the Mississippi River in Louisiana, used the alligator as their totem, or symbol of their tribe. The Atakapa people of Louisiana built large burial mounds that probably served as sacred places. One such mound was 600 feet (183 m) long and in the shape of an alligator.

For many ancient Chinese tribes, alligators were traditional symbols of good fortune, strength, and perseverance, and the animals were honored as representations of guardian spirits. Being timid creatures, Chinese alligators rarely had deadly encounters with humans and were not met with the same fear as American alligators.

People in the U.S. were both terrified by and fascinated with alligators, hunting them extensively as land was cleared and swamps were drained to make room for cities and houses, but also treating them like circus entertainment. The first public alligator farm opened in 1893 in St. Augustine, Florida, and countless others soon followed. Tourists were given the chance to see—and shoot—alligators from steamboats on river and swamp cruises, and alligator skins, teeth, and even live baby alligators became popular souvenirs of the American Southeast. In one instance, the famous French actress Sarah Bernhardt shipped a live alligator to Paris from Louisiana in 1900. Once released from its crate, the hungry alligator promptly ate Bernhardt's tiny terrier. The actress had the alligator shot and then hung its stuffed head on her wall.

In the 1920s, the Seminole Indians, who had lived in harmony with the alligators that flourished in the swamps and river valleys of Florida, became the first "gator wrestlers" in America, putting on special shows for eager spectators. Alligators cannot be trained, but their behavior can be safely predicted by experts who, to this day, straddle alligators and pet them into submission at such tourist attractions as Jungle Adventures Nature Park and Zoo in Christmas, Florida. At Gatorland in Kissimmee,

The Florida Gators won the 2009 College Bowl Championship Series to become national champions.

Proud of their native reptile, Floridians created the Gator Bowl in 1946, an annual college football game played in Jacksonville, Florida.

Attractions such as Florida's Gatorland feature alligators leaping for food during live shows.

Florida, alligators jump high out of the water to take food from the hands of expert alligator handlers.

Alligators quickly lose their fear of humans, though, especially when food is involved. By the time they are juveniles, they can be daring and aggressive. In fact, in every state where alligators live, the government has made it illegal to feed alligators in the wild. While alligators smaller than eight feet (2.4 m) long rarely attack humans, larger alligators may chase a human, bite repeatedly, and cause serious injury or even death.

There have been only about 400 alligator attacks in the U.S. since 1948. Fewer than 25 resulted in death, and most of those were from infection or blood loss, not from being consumed by the alligator. As more people move into common alligator habitats such as coastal areas and along inland waterways, chances that they will encounter alligators increase. While concrete and wooden fences around water will usually keep alligators where they belong, people have witnessed alligators climbing chain-link fences to reach prey, which, unfortunately, may be the family dog.

The abundance of alligators and the ease of raising them on farms aids in their **commercial** value. Alligator

Alligators use their powerful tails to thrust themselves out of the water in a vertical leap that is equal in height to their body length.

The alligator was one of four animals used to promote wildlife conservation on a set of 1971 stamps.

In the American Southeast, alligator feet and teeth are considered good luck charms, much as a rabbit's foot is regarded in other places.

fat was once used to make ink and to grease machines. Teeth, bones, and claws were sold as "magical remedies," and alligator meat was sold as a Southern delicacy. But it was the alligator's hide that was always most highly prized. Purses, shoes, boots, belts, and even saddles were made from alligator leather. In 1900, more than a quarter-million alligator hides were processed in the U.S., with about half of them coming from Florida and Louisiana.

Much of what people knew about alligators in the early 20th century can be attributed to E. A. McIlhenny's 1935 book *The Alligator's Life History*. Based upon his observations of alligators in his home state of Louisiana, the book became an early reference work on everything from alligator behavior to uses for alligator meat and skin.

The alligator's unique skin nearly cost the species its existence. By the 1960s, American alligators had been hunted nearly to **extinction**. When the U.S. government realized the threat, alligator hunting became illegal and, in 1967, the American alligator was officially listed as an endangered species. Research, rather than money or sport, became the new goal in tracking alligators throughout the American South.

Alligator **poaching** was vigorously prosecuted, and, within just 10 years, the overall population of American alligators had recovered. In 1976, limited hunting was allowed, and in 1983, alligators were no longer considered endangered. They were instead classified as "threatened for reasons of similarity in appearance." This means the sale of alligator skin, meat, and other products is strictly regulated so that other endangered alligator relatives are not disguised as alligators and sold illegally.

People can travel on airboats without damaging wetland habitat because the boats' propellers are above water.

The human imprint on lands near the Yangtze River has devastated Chinese alligators in recent decades.

AN AMAZING COMEBACK

Alligators are so abundant once again in Florida, Louisiana, and several other states that they are considered a **nuisance** in some communities and must be relocated. In Florida alone, about 6,000 alligators are relocated every year. The American alligator's comeback from the brink of extinction is a success story that researchers want to replicate, though, to help save its Chinese relative.

Due to habitat destruction, the Chinese alligator is one of the most endangered reptiles on the planet. Most of its wetland environment has been drained by dams to provide water for growing cities, especially along the Yangtze River, or converted to agricultural use for growing rice. Farmers consider the alligator a nuisance, and, despite laws designed to protect them, many alligators are trapped and shot each year. With fewer than 200 Chinese alligators left in the wild, **inbreeding** is a serious threat to their future as well. Scientists predict that the Chinese alligator will be extinct in the wild by 2025.

Although so few Chinese alligators remain in the wild, the species is thriving in captivity. The Chinese Alligator

Alligators nap lightly and can awaken at the slightest disturbance.

Alligators tunneling under riverbanks can damage levees, so researchers try to develop ways of keeping alligators out of such areas.

In order to save Chinese alligators, many are hatched at alligator research centers in China.

If an alligator loses the tip of its tail, the tail will regenerate, or regrow itself, as a firm but flexible tissue called cartilage.

Breeding and Research Center in the city of Xuancheng is home to 9,000 Chinese alligators—the largest group in the world. Another 1,000 are held at a research center in the city of Changxing. In America, Chinese alligators are currently bred at the Rockefeller Wildlife Refuge along Louisiana's Gulf Coast. Despite the damage caused by a series of hurricanes over the past several years and the closing of the refuge to the public, Chinese alligator research and breeding continues at the center and at the Houston Zoo in Texas.

In 2003, the Wildlife Conservation Society, which is headquartered in New York City, assisted in the first-ever release of **captive-reared** alligators in China's Anhui Province, the alligators' native habitat. Three alligators were fitted with radio transmitters and released. Students from East China Normal University monitored the alligators for one year. They learned that all three alligators survived, and at least one of the two females nested in 2004 and 2005. Perhaps one day the Chinese alligator will enjoy the same successful population recovery as its cousin.

With so many alligators in the southeastern U.S., state governments want to protect alligators from humans

ALLIGATOR ENCOUNTERS

I accordingly proceeded and made good my entrance into the lagoon, though not without opposition from the alligators, who formed a line across the entrance, but did not pursue me into it, nor was I molested by any there, though there were some very large ones in a cove at the upper end. I soon caught more trout than I had present occasion for, and the air was too hot and sultry to admit of their being kept for many hours, even though salted or barbecued. I now prepared for my return to camp, which I succeeded in with but little trouble, by keeping close to the shore, yet I was opposed upon re-entering the river out of the lagoon, and pursued near to my landing (though not closely attacked) particularly by an old daring one, about twelve feet in length, who kept close after me, and when I stepped on shore and turned about, in order to draw up my canoe, he rushed up near my feet and lay there for some time, looking me in the face, his head and shoulders out of water.

from Travels, *by William Bartram (1739–1823)*

Chemical gases released by industry collect in the atmosphere and become acid rain, polluting alligator habitats.

while at the same time protecting humans from alligators. They do this by funding educational programs that teach people about the vital role alligators play in wetland habitats and by instructing swimmers and boaters how to avoid conflicts with alligators.

To monitor the millions of American alligators living in Florida, Louisiana, and other southern states, researchers use a technique called "shining." Alligators spend their nights in the water and can easily be counted when a light is shone across their reflective eyes. Other research performed on alligators involves their eating and nesting habits, reproduction and growth, management of populations close to urban areas, and alligator capturing practices. But the greatest area of concern is how pollution affects alligators.

The University of Georgia at Athens conducts ongoing research on alligators that feed on prey living in coal ash basins in Georgia. Coal ash, a waste product of burning coal for electricity, contains high amounts of toxic chemicals. The ash spews from smokestacks at coal-burning facilities throughout the state and is carried through the atmosphere until it falls down to the earth again with rain and runs into low-lying areas called basins. Such pollution results in physical deformities and damage to the nervous systems of fish and frogs—two of the alligator's main food sources.

Other pollutants, such as toxic waste and heavy metals from industry run-off, **contaminate** alligator habitats. Scientists monitor both pollution levels and alligator populations to determine the effects of pollution on the living things in an area. Some studies involve tagging alligators with radio transmitters to track their movement. Researchers want to find out if alligators purposely travel from more polluted areas to less polluted ones.

Alligator farming—for skins and meat—is important to the **economies** of several states, including Louisiana, which has more than 100 licensed alligator farms, the most of any state. Researchers are continuously trying to improve farming methods by implementing changes in such things as the design of alligator farms. Because a large male alligator in a confined area can chase smaller alligators away from food, many alligator farms utilize channels instead of a single pond. Farmers have discovered that having several waterways separated by

A member of the Florida Alligator Trappers Association once described the flavor of alligator meat as a cross between chicken and lobster.

For the safety of both people and alligators, signs are posted near bodies of water frequented by alligators.

banks rather than a single open area gives alligators a sense of having more space and thus keeps one male from taking over. The channels actually encourage all of the alligators to get along and even pile on top of one another without fighting.

Alligator eggs are harvested from the wild to keep populations of farm-raised alligators from inbreeding. Wildlife management specialists routinely take about 50 percent of the eggs laid in designated areas where alligators nest. These eggs are then sold to alligator farms to replenish their stocks of alligators. Research on the impact that such egg removal has on alligator nesting habits is being conducted by various agencies in the Southeast, including the Florida Game and Fresh Water Fish Commission. So far, these studies have indicated that egg removal is not only harmless to alligator populations, but it encourages greater numbers of alligators to breed and nest.

Mark Merchant, a biochemist at McNeese State University in Louisiana, and Lancia Darville, a researcher at Louisiana State University in Baton Rouge, were the first people to publish research on alligator blood, which contains a substance that kills harmful bacteria. This

research could potentially result in the development of drugs that could treat deadly bacteria and infections—perhaps even the HIV virus that causes **AIDS**—by the year 2020.

For thousands of years, people's interest in alligators has ranged from fear to fascination to respect for alligators as a vital link in the wetland **food chain**. We still have much to learn about these remarkable reptiles and how their biological secrets can benefit us. But what is more important is discovering how we can help them continue to survive in the wild.

In 1987, Florida designated the American alligator as its official state reptile, promoting the animal's status.

ANIMAL TALE:
THE CHOCTAW HUNTERS

This Choctaw Indian legend tells how an alligator helped the Choctaw people of southern Mississippi become the greatest deer hunters in history, hunting responsibly and with respect for their brother animals.

Deep in a marshy forest near the Gulf of Mexico, a Choctaw man tried and tried but always failed at hunting. Each time he was about to shoot a deer, a bird would cry out and startle the deer, or the man would snap a twig and send the deer running. No matter what, his arrow always missed.

One day, the man walked deep into the swamp, vowing not to return home unless it was with a deer. After several days, he came upon a dry pit where there had once been water. There lay an enormous alligator. Having had no water for many days, the pitiful creature was near death.

The man said to the alligator, "Brother alligator, your luck is worse than mine."

In a weak voice, the alligator spoke: "I must find water, but I am too weak to travel. I know that you try and try, but the deer always escape your arrow. If you help me, I will make you a great hunter."

The man agreed, though he feared the alligator. "May I tie your legs together and tie your mouth shut so you cannot harm me?" he asked.

With a weak smile, the great alligator rolled onto its back. The man removed his belt and wrapped it around the alligator's mouth. He used vines to tie the alligator's legs together. Then he hoisted the alligator onto his shoulders and headed through the swamp.

After many hours, they reached a deep pool of water, and the man untied the alligator. With a happy groan, the alligator slid into the pool. "Thank you," the alligator said. "Now do as I say, and you will become a great hunter. Go into the forest with your bow and arrows. First, you will meet a sister doe. She will be small. She is too young, so you must not shoot her. Greet her and move on. Next you will meet a larger sister doe," the alligator continued. "She is a mother with fawns. She will have fawns each year for many years, so you must not shoot her. Greet her and move on." The man nodded.

Then the alligator said, "Next, you will meet a brother buck. He will not be very large. He is young and will father many fawns, so you must not shoot him. Greet him and move on." The man was puzzled, but he agreed to follow the alligator's instructions.

"Finally," said the alligator, "you will meet a larger brother buck. He will be tall and old. He has had a long life and will be ready to give it to you, so you may shoot him. Greet this buck and thank him for giving his life to you. Do all of this and you will be the greatest of all hunters."

The man bid the alligator farewell and went away to do as he was told. He met all the deer, but he shot only the old buck. Back in the village, everyone hailed him as the greatest of their hunters. Feasting on the deer meat, the man recounted to all of the other men what the wise alligator had told him. From then on, all the Choctaws hunted that way and became the greatest of deer hunters.

GLOSSARY

AIDS – a disease that causes the failure of many body systems and weakens the body's ability to fight off illness

aquatic – living or growing in water

captive-reared – raised in a place from which escape is not possible

commercial – used for business and to gain a profit rather than for personal reasons

contaminate – to negatively affect by exposure to a polluting substance

dermal – of or relating to the skin, which is also called dermis

economies – the wealth and resources of regions

extinction – the act or process of becoming extinct; coming to an end or dying out

food chain – a system in nature in which living things are dependent on each other for food

inbreeding – the mating of individuals that are closely related; it can result in having offspring with health problems

levees – mounds of earth or stone built to prevent the flooding of rivers

medieval – relating to the period of European history known as the Middle Ages, or the years A.D. 400 to 1450

nuisance – something annoying or harmful to people or the land

poaching – hunting protected species of wild animals, even though doing so is against the law

solitary – alone, without companions

vertebrates – animals that have a backbone, including mammals, birds, reptiles, amphibians, and fish

webbed – connected by a web (of skin, as in the case of webbed feet)

SELECTED BIBLIOGRAPHY

Alderton, David. *Crocodiles and Alligators of the World.* New York: Facts on File, 2004.

Florida Fish and Wildlife Conservation Commission. "Alligator Management." http://myfwc.com/gators.

Glasgow, Vaughn L. *A Social History of the American Alligator: The Earth Trembles with His Thunder.* New York: St. Martin's Press, 1991.

Grenard, Steve. *Handbook of Alligators and Crocodiles.* Malabar, Fla.: Krieger Publishing Company, 1991.

Jacksonville Zoo and Gardens. "Biofacts: The American Alligator." http://www.jaxzoo.org/animals/biofacts/AmericanAlligator.asp.

Lockwood, C. C. *The Alligator Book.* Baton Rouge: Louisiana State University Press, 2002.

Every year, about half a million people visit Everglades National Park in Florida to see alligators in the wild.

INDEX